Our
Pennsylvania

Photography by Jerry Irwin

Voyageur Press

First published in 2003 by Voyageur Press, an imprint of MBI Publishing Company, Galtier Plaza, Suite 200, 380 Jackson Street, St. Paul, MN 55101-3885 USA

MBI Publishing Company titles are also available at discounts in bulk quantity for industrial or sales-promotional use. For details write to Special Sales Manager at MBI Publishing Company, Galtier Plaza, Suite 200, 380 Jackson Street, St. Paul, MN 55101-3885 USA

Printed in Hong Kong

Library of Congress Cataloging-in-Publication Data available
ISBN-13: 978-0-89658-554-6
ISBN-10: 0-89658-554-9

Page 1: *Fall color spills through the Allegheny National Forest.*

Page 2: *In Lancaster County, Amish and Mennonite farmers plow fields with horse teams.*

Page 3: *The fertile valley farmland of central Pennsylvania unrolls in a patchwork of green and gold.*

Page 4, top: *Visitors ride the rails at the Steamtown National Historic Site in Scranton.*

Page 4, bottom: *Highrises of various heights and architectural styles make up Pittsburgh's compact downtown area.*

Page 5: *Pennsylvania's grand State Capitol building in Harrisburg was modeled after St. Peter's Basilica in Rome.*

Page 6: *The privately owned Great Valley Mill, a nineteenth-century grist mill in Paoli, is on the National Register of Historic Places.*

Page 7: *A Civil War cannon stands guard over the Gettysburg battlefield.*

Facing page: *White on white, a church in Germania nestles among the snowy trees.*

Dedication

For Janice, who shares my love for travel and adventure, and in loving memory of Joe Coyle, who showed me all the hidden corners. —JI

Above: *Many barns in Pennsylvania Dutch country are decorated with hex signs. These symbols were originally believed to ward off evil and attract good fortune; today they are regarded mainly as colorful examples of folk art.*

Right: *The north-central farm country blazes with color in the fall.*

The sloping roof of a round dairy barn northeast of Gettysburg echoes the rolling shape of the hills on which it stands.

Above: *Traffic slows to a leisurely saunter during rural rush hour.*

Overleaf: *A farmstead and fields stretch out along a verdant ridge in Tioga County. Nine million acres of Pennsylvania are farmland.*

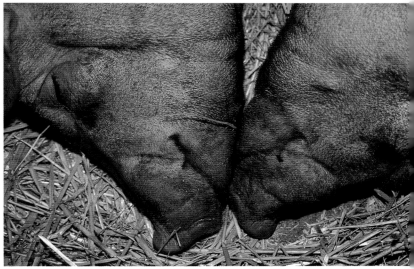

Left: *With its sturdy stone foundation, this classic, red-sided barn has stood the test of time in rural Berks County. Pennsylvania's barn styles recall those of Germany and England, the native lands of the state's first European settlers.*

Above: *Two pigs share a snooze in the straw.*

Top: *Colorful jars of pickles, peppers, and relish, and baskets of potatoes and tomatoes invite drivers to stop at roadside produce stands and share the harvest.*

Above: *The midway rides of the Perry County Fair create a whirling stream of light. Seven million people total attend Pennsylvania's various county and community fairs each year.*

Right: *Founded by immigrants from Bavaria, the little town of St. Mary's celebrates its heritage with an annual August polka festival.*

Left: *Tobacco is one of the state's leading farm products, along with dairy products, mushrooms, apples, grapes, peaches, and cut flowers.*

Facing page: *Perhaps because of their bucolic setting, even the most modern farms in Pennsylvania have a timeless quality about them.*

Above: *County fairs give classic tractor buffs a chance to show off their restoration projects. Some machines are only for show; some are used to demonstrate old-time farming techniques; and some compete in races, pulls, and other contests.*

Stone and brick barns, like this gable-roofed horse barn in Chester County, were a sign of prosperity and wealth on early farms, since only farmers with deep pockets could afford for expert stonemasons to build them.

Top: *Forkville's annual Sleigh Rally features driving contests, obstacle courses, an antique sleigh exhibit, and, of course, sleigh rides through the Appalachian Mountains.*

Above: *The heart of any farm is its barn, and in many cases, the barn was much larger than the family farmhouse. It is likely that the wings of this large red barn were added at different times, as the farmer's operation and financial resources grew.*

Both pages: *Farming is the foundation of the Plain People communities of southeastern Pennsylvania. On Old Order Amish and Mennonite farms, the whole family helps with the chores, from spring planting to daily milking.*

Both photos: *The teachings of Old Order churches stress cooperation and love for one's neighbors. Seven hundred men came from as far as Ohio, New York, and Lancaster County to help communities in Crawford County rebuild barns and other structures destroyed by a tornado.*

Facing page: *A wheat field spreads out between two neat plots of green corn on an Amish farmstead in Paradise township.*

27

The sounds of horses hooves and buggy wheels on gravel carry along the quiet roads around Sugar Grove in Warren County.

Many Old Order farmers have blended aspects of the modern world into their traditional way of life. This family, for instance, is using a team of horses to power a mechanical hay baler.

Left: *A sixteen-year-old Amish girl adjusts her prayer cap.*

Below: *Plain People dress conservatively to demonstrate their decision to be separate from the larger world. Hats, solid blue shirts, suspenders, ankle-length dresses, and aprons are common attire.*

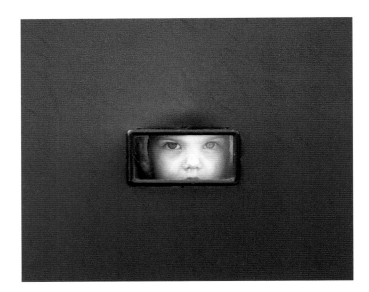

Right: *Mennonite buggies can be recognized by their black tops. Amish buggies may also have black tops, but the tops may also be gray, yellow, white, or even orange, depending on the settlement they belong to.*

Below: *A line of austere buggies waits in the farmyard while Old Order Amish families attend the weekly worship service.*

In winter, a sleigh makes for smooth riding over snow-covered country lanes.

A ride along the back roads of Somerset County seems to transport travelers to an earlier time in American history, when everyone rode in horse-drawn buggies and mighty mills were still in operation.

The White Rock Bridge is one of twenty-eight covered bridges in Lancaster County. Pennsylvania has more than 200 covered bridges—more than any other state—but at one time it had more than 1,500.

This barn-red bridge crosses Laurel Hill Creek in Somerset County. The roof and walls of a covered bridge protect the wood of the bridge itself from the effects of weather.

Left: *The covered bridge in McConnell's Mill State Park spans Slippery Rock Creek. Behind it stands the park's namesake, the restored grist mill.*

Below: *Cows and kids wade in Octoraro Creek beneath the Jackson's Mill Bridge.*

Mist softens the view of Erie County's Gudgeonville Bridge and the tranquil waters of Elk Creek.

Winding up over bluffs and down into valleys, Pennsylvania's country roads frequently offer spectacular overviews of the landscape.

A stone farmhouse falls into picturesque decay in the woodlands of Chester County.

Apple blossoms add a layer of lacy white to the lush green of Adams County valleys.

Top: *The Pennsylvania countryside is dotted with small, comely churches in various denominations. The East Point Ebenezer Church stands atop a bluff in Tioga County.*

Above: *Giving new meaning to the term "mobile home," an old, three-story, brick farmhouse takes to the road on its way to a new site in Chester County.*

All photos: *The Pennsylvania country-side is just as scenic in the winter as in the spring and fall. Snow turns the state's farmsteads and lanes into a winter wonderland, just waiting for the sleigh, sled, and ski.*

In the Appalachian Ridge region, the terrain is mountainous, with fertile valleys and plateaus in between.

Charming Wellsboro—with its town square, courthouse, gas lights, and Victorian houses— is a classic American small town.

Top: *Old stone bridges, such as this one near Mount Joy, still carry traffic across waterways in many small towns.*

Above: *The historic town of Liverpool has fewer than one thousand residents.*

Right: *The Thomas Beaver Free Library in Danville has welcomed readers since 1886.*

Below: *The faded sign of a long-gone store adds to the nostalgic charm of Mansfield's Main Street.*

Facing page: *A statue of native son Andrew Gregg Curtin, Pennsylvania's governor from 1861 to 1867, stands in front of the Centre County Courthouse in Bellefonte.*

Above: *Located along the Monongahela River, Brownsville first prospered as a steamboat landing. In the 1800s, it became a railroad and commercial center as the steel industry tapped the region's coal veins for fuel. Today the town attracts visitors with its well-preserved historic sites.*

Facing page: *Formerly named Mauch Chunk, the town of Jim Thorpe adopted its current name in honor of the famous athlete.*

Above: *Built in the nineteenth century, the Strasburg Rail Road had fallen into disuse by the 1950s, when a group of volunteers restored it to its original glory. Today, the train carries visitors on scenic tours of the Amish farm country between the towns of Strasburg and Paradise.*

Facing page: *The dramatic Tunkhannock Viaduct—also known as the Nicholson Bridge—is the world's longest concrete railroad bridge. It is 300 feet high at its tallest point, 2,375 feet long, and only 34 feet wide.*

Top: *Listed on the National Register of Historic Places, the Classical Revival–style Bradford County Courthouse looms over Main Street in the river town of Towanda.*

Right: *The regal, red-brick Venango County Courthouse stands as a testament to the wealth that the oil boom brought to northwest Pennsylvania in the late-nineteenth century.*

For three days in 1863, the town of Gettysburg was filled with the sounds of battle between Union and Confederate soldiers in what would be the turning point of the Civil War. Today the town is nearly surrounded by Gettysburg National Military Park.

The U.S. Congress set aside Gettysburg National Military Park in 1895 as a memorial to the armies that fought the epic three-day battle. The park comprises almost 6,000 acres.

58

Facing page: *Gettysburg National Military park includes 1,400 monuments, markers, and memorials.*

Above: *President Abraham Lincoln wrote the "Gettysburg Address" for the November 1863 dedication ceremony of Gettysburg National Cemetery, a burial ground for Union soldiers.*

Every summer, thousands of dedicated re-enactors at Gettysburg National Military Park relive the events of the eponymous Civil War battle. The re-enactments are part of several living history activities at the park.

Left: *At Valley Forge National Historic Park, costumed actors re-create the lives of the soldiers of George Washington's Continental Army, who endured the long winter of 1777–1778 there.*

Below: *British soldiers fire their muskets at the Continental Army during an annual re-enactment of the Revolutionary War battle fought at Brandywine.*

A city of bridges, Pittsburgh stands at the point where the Allegheny and Monongahela Rivers join to form the Ohio River.

The forty-two-story Cathedral of Learning (left) stands at the heart of the University of Pittsburgh campus. Nearby is the college's neo-Gothic Heinz Chapel.

Facing page: *The Duquesne Incline uses nineteenth-century cable cars to lift sightseers to the top of Mount Washington for an overview of downtown Pittsburgh.*

Above: *The Pittsburgh Pirates played their first game in PNC Park in 2001. The two-deck ballpark is located on the shore of the Allegheny River.*

Above: *Row houses perch along the steep Pittsburgh hillsides.*

Facing page: *Pittsburgh's Pennsylvania Railroad station was completed in 1901, before the "h" was added to the city's name.*

Right: *Visitors enjoy the blooms in one of Longwood Gardens' twenty indoor gardens. Located thirty miles from Philadelphia, the horticultural showcase also includes twenty outdoor gardens.*

Below: *The Saint Nicholas Chapel in Beaver County was modeled after the Russian Orthodox churches of Eastern Europe.*

Fallingwater is considered one of architect Frank Lloyd Wright's most magnificent works. The home was designed to blend harmoniously with the nature of the Laurel Highlands.

JAMES M. STEWART
DEDICATED MAY 21 1983
ON THE OCCASION OF JIMMY'S
75TH BIRTHDAY CELEBRATION

Facing page: *The town of Indiana pays tribute to its most famous son at the Jimmy Stewart Museum.*

Left: *The collections at the Mercer Museum in Doylestown focus on the history of Bucks County, everyday life in pre-industrial America, and the museum's millionaire namesake, Henry Mercer.*

Below: *The home and studio of painter and illustrator N. C. Wyeth, preserved at the Brandywine River Museum in Chadds Ford, gives visitors a glimpse into the artist's creative world.*

Flags and mementos mark the September 11, 2001, crash site of United Airlines Flight 93, north of Shanksville.

In May 1889, Johnstown was devastated by a flood when a dam north of the town collapsed. Many of the flood's 2,209 victims, including 777 unidentified victims, are buried in Grandview Cemetery.

Left: *When the Nittany Lions football team scores a touch-down, the roar is deafening. That's because Beaver Stadium at Penn State University can hold more than 107,000 fans.*

Above: *The Penn State cheerleading squad works the sidelines during a game.*

The trees and ground become nothing but a blur during a high-flying Roto-Jets ride at Knoebels Amusement Park.

Left: *Hershey's Chocolate World, the visitors center for the Hershey Foods Corporation, is often the first stop for chocolate lovers making pilgrimages to the town of Hershey.*

Below: *Lighter-shaped street lights line the drive up to the Zippo/Case Visitors Center, a museum tracing the history of Zippo lighters and Case pocket-knives.*

Left: *The Brandywine Scenic Railroad carries visitors on a winding ride through the southeastern Pennsylvania countryside.*

Above: *The Railroad Museum of Pennsylvania displays a large collection of railroad artifacts and more than a hundred locomotives and cars.*

Right: *The magnificent interior of the State Capitol dome is a work of art.*

Below: *Edwin Drake drilled the world's first successful oil well in Titusville in 1859. The Drake Well Museum commemorates this birth-place of the petroleum industry.*

Facing page: *The sky above Shawnee-on-Delaware fills with colorful hot air balloons during the town's annual October festival.*

Left: *The brilliant lights of Philadelphia's Center City reflect on the waters of the Schuylkill River.*

Above: *At 945 feet in height and sixty-one stories, Liberty Place One (left) towers above the rest of the skyline. Liberty Place Two, next door, is slightly shorter.*

From its perch in Fairmount Park, the Philadelphia Museum of Art overlooks the Schuylkill River. Below the museum stands a collection of nineteenth-century buildings that comprise the former waterworks.

Boathouse Row, a collection of Victorian buildings, houses the sculls of local rowing clubs.

Both photos: *Independence Hall and the Liberty Bell are both part of Independence National Historic Park, forty-five acres of national history in the heart of a bustling modern city. The park attracts almost three million visitors per year.*

Elfreth's Alley is the oldest residential street in the country. The first houses were built in 1713, and many are still private residences today. The street is still paved with ankle-turning cobblestones.

Left: *A statue of William Penn, the state's founder and namesake, looks down from the pinnacle of Philadelphia's City Hall.*

Below: *Built in 1786, the Physick House on Philadelphia's Society Hill earned its name as the residence of Dr. Philip Syng Physick, known as the "Father of American Surgery," who lived in the townhouse from 1815 to 1837.*

Blue sky and high clouds accentuate the view of the jagged Philadelphia skyline.

Cheese, olives, and vinegar are just some of the fragrant gourmet goods lining the main aisle of Di Bruno Brothers Italian market.

All photos: *The ethnic diversity of Philadelphia comes alive with a variety of cultural festivals, including the African-American street festival of Odunde; the Chinese New Year parade in Chinatown; and the Festival of India at Penn's Landing.*

Swann Memorial Fountain in Logan Circle was designed by Alexander Stirling Calder, son Alexander Milne Calder, who designed the statue of William Penn that tops City Hall, in the background.

Left: *Some 15,000 people take part in Philadelphia's famous New Year's Day Mummers Parade, a tradition dating back more than one hundred years. Thousands of spectators line up along the streets to watch the fun.*

Below: *Considering that Philadelphia is the birthplace of the nation, it is no surprise the city puts on a fantastic Fourth of July parade.*

Right: *It takes dexterity, athleticism, and teamwork to win at a double Dutch jump rope competition.*

Below: *More than 2,000 murals decorate the walls of Philadelphia neighborhoods. The murals hide graffiti, add color to the city, and foster a sense of community.*

The businesses on funky, eclectic South Street attract plenty of traffic.

Above and facing page, bottom: *Pennsylvanians connect with the Great Lake Erie via the beaches at Presque Isle State Park.*

Left: *Presque Isle Light is an active station, but its light has been automated since 1944. No longer needed for a lightkeeper, the red-brick house is now home to employees of the Presque Isle State Park.*

Overleaf: *As it crosses the 301-foot-tall, steel Kinzua Bridge, an excursion train offers a breathtaking view of the fall foliage in Allegheny National Forest.*

In autumn hardwood trees turn the back roads of Allegheny National Forest into tunnels of gold.

Left: *Some of the hemlock, beech, and white pine trees in Hearts Content Recreation Area are 300 to 400 years old.*

Below: *Whitetail deer are abundant in Pennsylvania woodlands.*

Left and below: *Quiet trails invite hikers and nature-lovers to explore the 513,257 acres of Allegheny National Forest, the only national forest in Pennsylvania.*

Facing page: *Hikers along the Appalachian Trail take a break and enjoy the view from Pinnacle Overlook.*

Facing page and below: *Most of Pennsylvania's trees are deciduous hardwoods, such as maple, birch, beech, oak, sycamore, ash, hickory, walnut, and poplar. The leaves of these trees turn brilliant colors before dropping in the fall.*

Left: *Pennsylvania has nearly 17 million acres of forest land, the ideal habitat for wild turkeys and other game birds.*

Forested hillsides meet the splendor of blue water along the banks of the Allegheny Reservoir in Warren County.

Both photos: *Rafters and kayakers tackle the whitewater in the scenic Lehigh River Gorge.*

Facing page: *Pine Creek is a haven for trout and the anglers who seek them.*

Left and below: *The fall foliage in Pine Creek Gorge—the Grand Canyon of Pennsylvania—is stunning from any angle. The gorge is fifty miles long, 1,000 feet deep, covered in evergreen and hardwood trees, and a laced by network of scenic hiking trails.*

Overleaf: *Calm waters reflect the lakeside cottages at the Nine-Mile Motel in Potter County.*

Early June wildflowers carpet the banks of Pine Creek in Lycoming County.

With its mountains and natural areas, Pennsylvania is a hiker's paradise. The Mid-State Trail takes intrepid backpackers to Gillespie Point for a stunning overview of Pine Creek Gorge.

When New Yorkers and Bostonians want to escape the city, many head to Pennsylvania's Pocono Mountains. The steep mountain range along the state's New Jersey border is especially popular as a skiing and honeymoon destination.

Each year, bird watchers flock to Hawk Mountain Sanctuary on Kittatinny Ridge between September and November to see raptors migrating along the Appalachian Flyway.

Above: *Some of the white pines and hemlocks in Cook Forest State Park are three feet in diameter, almost 200 feet tall, and more than 350 years old. These old-growth forests were some of the same trees that formed "Penn's Woods," the original Pennsylvania settlement.*

Right: *Ricketts Glen State Park, regarded as one of the state's most scenic natural areas, includes twenty-two named waterfalls.*

Overleaf: *The mighty Susquehanna River wends though the Appalachian Mountains and some of the state's richest farmland.*

For a breathtaking overview of the northern Susquehanna River, visit Wyalusing Rocks in Bradford County (above). Or take in the southernmost leg of the river from Pinnacle Overlook in Lancaster County (facing page).

Left: *Visitors look north over the Appalachian Trail from an overlook at Blue Rocks.*

Above: *The wide Delaware River carves a valley along the eastern edge of the Pocono Mountains. The wild, scenic beauty of the valley is protected by the Delaware Water Gap National Recreation Area.*

Right: *Winter falls peacefully on the Allegheny National Forest. The forest covers about 800 square miles—an area nearly the size of Rhode Island.*

Below: *The resident elk herd of Elk County can be seen roaming near the town of Benezette.*